I0794828

On a Mat

by Tameron Dennis
illustrated by Mark Corcoran

Core Decodable 8

Mc Graw Hill Education

Bothell, WA • Chicago, IL • Columbus, OH • New York, NY

MHEonline.com

Copyright © 2015 McGraw-Hill Education

All rights reserved. No part of this publication may be reproduced or distributed in any form or by any means, or stored in a database or retrieval system, without the prior written consent of McGraw-Hill Education, including, but not limited to, network storage or transmission, or broadcast for distance learning.

Send all inquiries to:
McGraw-Hill Education
8787 Orion Place
Columbus, OH 43240

ISBN: 978-0-02-145282-8
MHID: 0-02-145282-2

Printed in the United States of America.

7 8 9 LCR 25 24 23

Tam

Tam on a mat

Sam

Sam on a mat

Matt

Matt on a mat

I am on a mat.

Sam sat on Tam.

Matt sat on Sam.

I sat on Matt.

Tam sat.

Tam sat on a mat.

Tam sat. Sam sat. Matt sat.

I sat on a mat.